THE HUMAN MACHINE

CELLS, TISSUES, AND ORGANS

Richard Spilsbury

www.heinemann.co.uk/library
Visit our website to find out more information about **Heinemann Library** books.

To order:
 Phone 44 (0)1865 888066
 Send a fax to 44 (0)1865 314091
 Visit the Heinemann Bookshop at www.heinemann.co.uk/library to browse our catalogue and order online.

First published in Great Britain by Heinemann, Halley Court, Jordan Hill, Oxford, OX2 8EJ, part of Harcourt Education.
Heinemann is a registered trademark of Harcourt Education Ltd.

Editorial: Nancy Dickmann and Rachel Howells
Design: Victoria Bevan and AMR Design Ltd
Illustrations: Medi-mation
Picture Research: Hannah Taylor
Production: Vicki Fitzgerald

Originated by Chroma
Printed and bound in China by CTPS

ISBN 978 0 431 19203 1 (hardback)
12 11 10 09 08
10 9 8 7 6 5 4 3 2 1

British Library Cataloguing in Publication Data
Spilsbury, Richard, 1963-
Cells, tissues, and organs. - (The human machine)
1. Cytology - Juvenile literature 2. Histology - Juvenile literature 3. Organs (Anatomy) - Juvenile literature
I. Title
611'.018
A full catalogue record for this book is available from the British Library.

Acknowledgements
The publishers would like to thank the following for permission to reproduce photographs: ©Alamy pp. **10** (Alan Schein), **5** (Stockbyte Platinum); ©Corbis pp. **4** (Alan Schein Photography), **27** (Jutta Klee), **22** (Najlah Feanny), **19** (Scott McDermott); ©Getty Images pp. **15** (DAGOC), **26** (Iconica), **21** (Stone); ©iStockphoto p. **29** (Justin Horrocks); ©Photolibrary p. **25** (Phototake Inc); ©Science Photo Library pp. **12** (Andrew Syred), **24** (Dr P. Marazzi), **17** (Herve Conge, ISM), **20** (Ian Hooton), **8** (K.R. Porter), **16** (Manfred Kage, Peter Arnold INC.), **18** (Paul Duda), **28** (Roger Harris), **9** (Skyscan), **7** (Steve Gschmeissner)

Cover photograph of fibroblast cells reproduced with permission of ©Science Photo Library/ Dr Torsten Wittmann.

The publishers would like to thank David Wright for his assistance in the preparation of this book.

Every effort has been made to contact copyright holders of any material reproduced in this book. Any omissions will be rectified in subsequent printings if notice is given to the publishers.

Contents

Any words appearing in the text in bold, **like this**, are explained in the glossary.

What are cells?

The human body, like that of any living thing, is made of tiny building blocks called **cells**. Cells make up our hair, skin, eyes, bones, muscles, stomach, and everything else inside and outside the body.

Think of an enormous building, such as a skyscraper, made of bricks. Cells are a bit like the bricks, because each makes up a tiny part of the whole. There are so many cells and they are so small that people cannot count them. However, each person is probably made up of tens of billions of cells!

What cells do

Cells do not only provide the structure of the different parts of our bodies. They also carry out the different jobs, or processes, that keep us alive. For example, cells let us release the **energy** we need from food. They also protect us from **germs** that could make us sick. Cells come in different shapes and sizes.

Cells are the building blocks which make up the human machine, similar to how bricks make up a building.

To grow from a baby to an adult, the number of cells in our bodies increases.

Growing

Are you taller and stronger than last year? Most living things grow and develop, or change, throughout their lives. To make a building taller, builders add more bricks. For any living thing to grow it must produce more cells. Most cells can simply **divide**, or split in two, to increase in number.

WHAT CELLS ARE MADE OF

Cells are small but they are made of even smaller building blocks called atoms. Atoms are the smallest units of matter. Unlike cells, atoms are not alive. But they make up everything in the world, from oceans and aeroplanes to sheep and MP3 players, whether it is living or not.

How do cells work?

Like a tiny factory, a cell is made up of different parts that each do their bit to keep the cell working properly.

Inside a cell

If you look at them through a microscope, most human cells look a bit like floppy bags filled with clear liquid. The jelly-like liquid is called the **cytoplasm**. The cytoplasm is made of water and various chemicals needed by the cell. Bubbles in the cytoplasm called vacuoles keep useful substances such as food, or waste the cell needs to get rid of, separate from the cytoplasm.

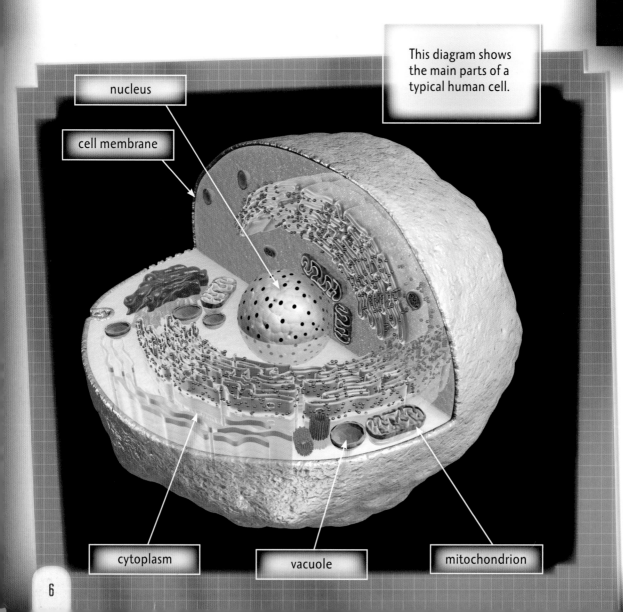

This diagram shows the main parts of a typical human cell.

nucleus

cell membrane

cytoplasm

vacuole

mitochondrion

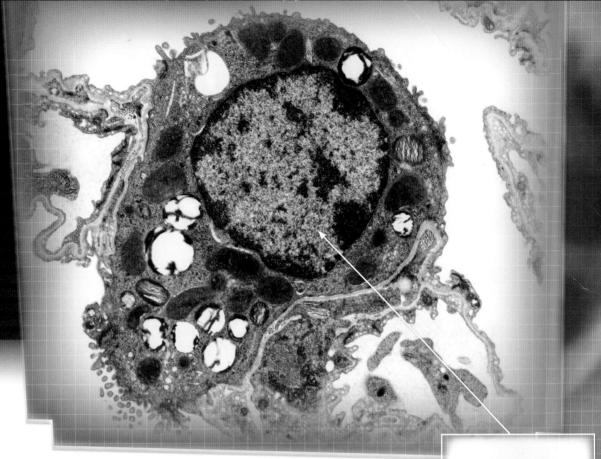

A real cell looks mostly transparent apart from the dark dot of the nucleus.

Dotted throughout the cytoplasm are **organelles** of different shapes. These are like different departments of the cell factory, each with a special purpose. Thin threads called filaments in the cytoplasm hold organelles in position within the cell.

At the centre

The biggest organelle, the **nucleus**, acts rather like a cell's main computer. The nucleus contains thin threads called **chromosomes**. They are like instruction manuals for the cell. The instructions show the cell what its job is for the body. The nucleus is surrounded by a **nuclear membrane**, a thin "skin" that allows substances to pass in and out.

PLANT CELLS

Plants are made of cells that are a little different to animal cells such as ours. For example, they have green parts called chloroplasts in the cytoplasm. These are where plants make their food using the Sun's energy. Animals eat food, so they do not have these organelles. Plant cells also have stiff cell walls around the outside that help them keep their shape.

Power for cells

All body functions, from moving muscles to thinking thoughts, rely on cells working. Work requires energy to make it happen. The organelles that release energy from food are called **mitochondria**. Some cells only have a few but others, such as those in muscles, have many mitochondria. This is because they need lots of energy to do their job.

A single mitochondrion is sausage-shaped on the outside and has little folds on the inside. The folds are where a mitochondrion releases energy. The process of releasing energy from food is called **respiration**.

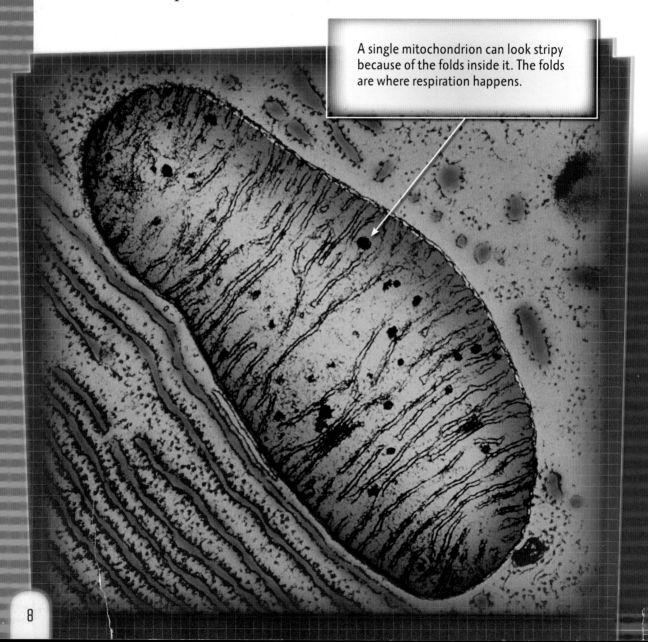

A single mitochondrion can look stripy because of the folds inside it. The folds are where respiration happens.

Respiration

Real power stations make heat energy by combining **oxygen** and fuel such as coal. Mitochondria make energy using **glucose** from food as fuel and oxygen that we breathe in. Both of these raw materials collect in the cytoplasm. Respiration also produces water and **carbon dioxide**. Water is useful to cells but carbon dioxide is poisonous when it builds up, so the cells get rid of it.

People burn fuel in power stations to make the energy we use in our homes, schools, and other places. Mitochondria are a bit like tiny power stations dotted throughout our bodies.

HEAT GENERATION

Respiration releases some energy as heat. Our bodies use this heat from mitochondria to provide a constant internal temperature of 37°C (98.6°F). We need this heat for cell processes to continue normally.

Cell membrane

All cells are enclosed by a **cell membrane**. This thin layer of fat holds in the cytoplasm and organelles in the same way that a plastic bag holds its contents. The cell membrane is the barrier between the cell and the watery fluid surrounding it. It can control what goes in and out. It lets in useful substances from outside the membrane, such as glucose. It keeps out germs, such as **bacteria**, that can be harmful.

Barriers at a metro station only let people through who have got a ticket. The cell membrane only lets through substances that it recognizes as useful.

CELL DEFENDERS

Bacteria and other cell invaders can punch a hole in cell membranes to let themselves in. They can then damage or destroy the cell, increase in number, and affect the health of a person's whole body. Cells form membranes around invaders and these join up with organelles called lysosomes. Strong chemicals inside lysosomes dissolve the unwanted visitors!

Moving through membranes

Substances move through the membrane in one of three ways. Some substances such as oxygen move straight through any part of the cell membrane by **diffusion**. This is when the substance travels from a place that has a lot of that substance to another place where there is less of it. Other substances can only get through small holes in the membrane that act as gates. Water easily moves through the gates by a special type of diffusion called **osmosis**. Water moves from where it is plentiful outside the cell to where there is less inside the cell. Other substances, such as glucose, are transported through the gates by special **proteins** in the membrane.

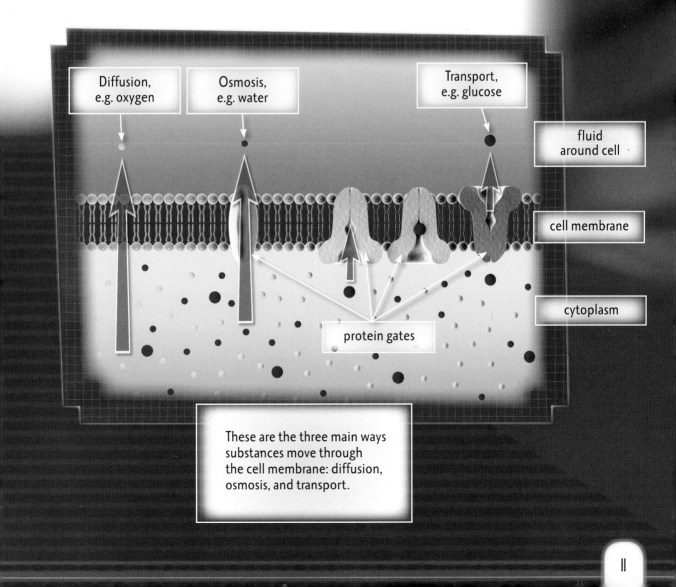

Diffusion, e.g. oxygen

Osmosis, e.g. water

Transport, e.g. glucose

fluid around cell

cell membrane

cytoplasm

protein gates

These are the three main ways substances move through the cell membrane: diffusion, osmosis, and transport.

Why do we need new cells?

We need new cells to replace those that are worn out. We also need them as building blocks when body parts such as muscles grow.

Dead cells

Like all living things, cells wear out and die. Cells can also be destroyed when you get injured. Dead skin cells flake off and add to household dust. Dead cells from inside your body are broken up or pass out with waste. Some dead cells stay in place. For example, our nails are made of hard layers of dead cells that protect the cells underneath from damage!

These are dead skin cells magnified hundreds of times. In one minute, normally about three billion cells in your body die.

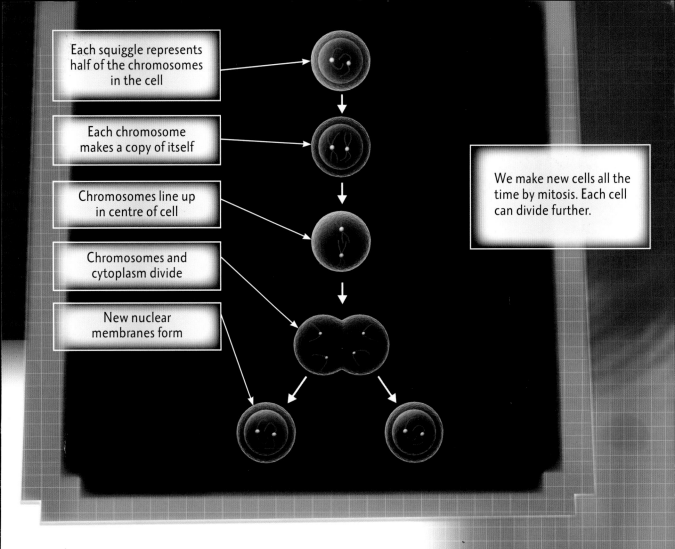

Each squiggle represents half of the chromosomes in the cell

Each chromosome makes a copy of itself

Chromosomes line up in centre of cell

Chromosomes and cytoplasm divide

New nuclear membranes form

We make new cells all the time by mitosis. Each cell can divide further.

Making new cells

The body makes new cells by **mitosis**. This is when one cell makes an exact copy of itself and divides into two identical cells. One skin cell would become two skin cells and each of these can make two cells and so on.

Mitosis starts when the chromosomes make copies of themselves. This causes the nucleus to swell up. The nuclear membrane then disappears and the swollen nucleus splits in two. Each half of the nucleus has a complete set of chromosomes. The nuclei move to opposite sides of the cell and the cell divides in two.

LIFESPAN OF CELLS

Some cells wear out more quickly than others. Those in the stomach lining last just two days, but those in your blood last four months. The longest lasting cells are in your brain. These survive up to 50 years (or more) but they are not replaced when they are worn out. This is why it is vital to protect your brain from damage, for example by wearing a helmet when cycling.

What are tissues?

You are an individual but you may also be part of a football team or maths club. Each person in a team works together to do a single job. Each cell has an individual job to do, too, but does not work alone. Individual cells are organized into teams of similar cells that work together. These cell groups are called **tissues**.

There are many different types of tissue, such as bone tissue made of bone cells and blood tissue containing blood cells. Different tissues usually have different shaped cells to help them do their job. For example, **neurons**, or nerve cells, are very long and narrow. They connect together rather like a network of wires to carry electrical messages from all parts of your body to and from your brain.

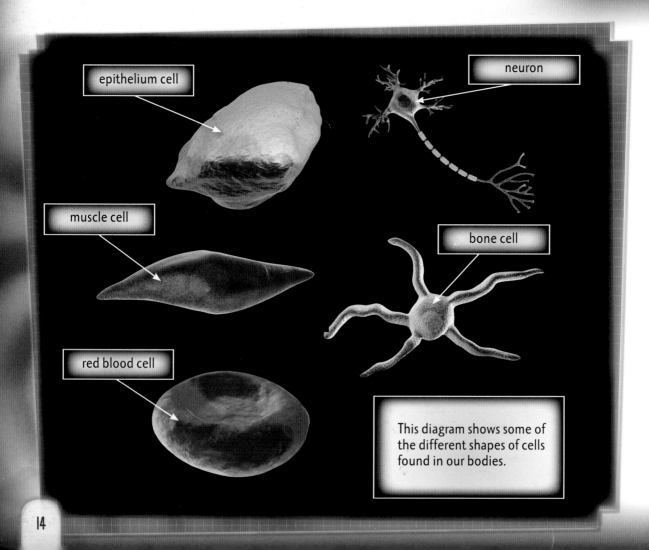

epithelium cell

neuron

muscle cell

bone cell

red blood cell

This diagram shows some of the different shapes of cells found in our bodies.

Gymnasts train to develop strong muscles so they can move with power and control.

Muscle tissue

Muscle tissue is made of stretchy muscle cells that can change shape. One example is the muscle cells in leg muscles, which are tube-shaped and grouped in bundles. Muscle bundles shorten in length to pull on leg bones and move them around. Muscle tissue in your intestines is made of shorter cells arranged in layers. This tissue squeezes **digested** or broken-down food through the centre of the intestine.

ONE OR MANY?

Most types of living things, from ants to giant redwood trees, are made of many cells and tissues. However, some types are made of just one cell. An amoeba is a one-celled animal that can move around and hunt for food in pond water.

15

Blood

Blood is the only liquid tissue. It contains three types of cells. **Red blood cells** give blood its red colour. They are the shape of a ball squashed in the middle and are about half the size of muscle cells. The only job of red blood cells is to transport gases around the body. They collect oxygen from the lungs and unload it at cells. They collect some of the waste carbon dioxide produced by the cells and take this to the lungs to be breathed out.

White blood cells are fewer in number in the blood. Their job is to get rid of living things such as bacteria that have got into blood, for example through wounds.

Platelets are smaller than red blood cells and act as the blood's repair kit. They group together at wounds, forming clots to patch up damaged blood vessels.

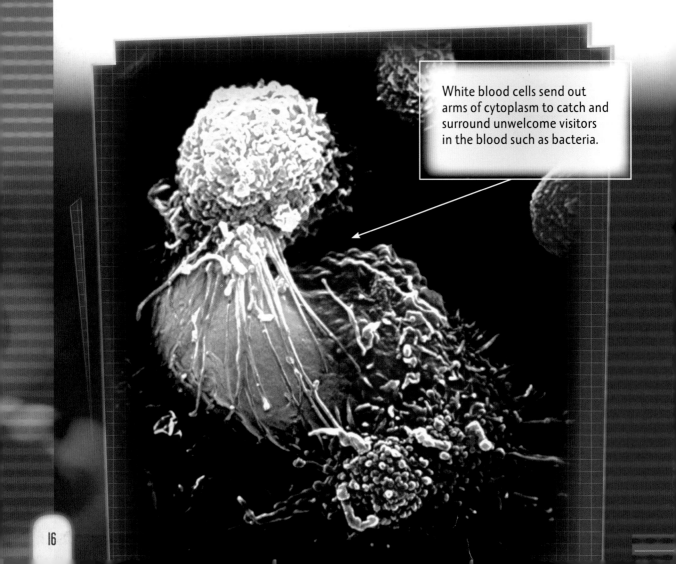

White blood cells send out arms of cytoplasm to catch and surround unwelcome visitors in the blood such as bacteria.

Bone and cartilage

Bone and **cartilage** are tissues that provide support and strength for our bodies. Bone makes up our skeletons and cartilage makes more flexible parts such as the nose and the tips of the ears. Both of these tissues are made of cells surrounded by other non-living substances. Rings of hard calcium in bone make it strong and rigid. Strands of a rubbery substance called collagen between cartilage cells make it flexible.

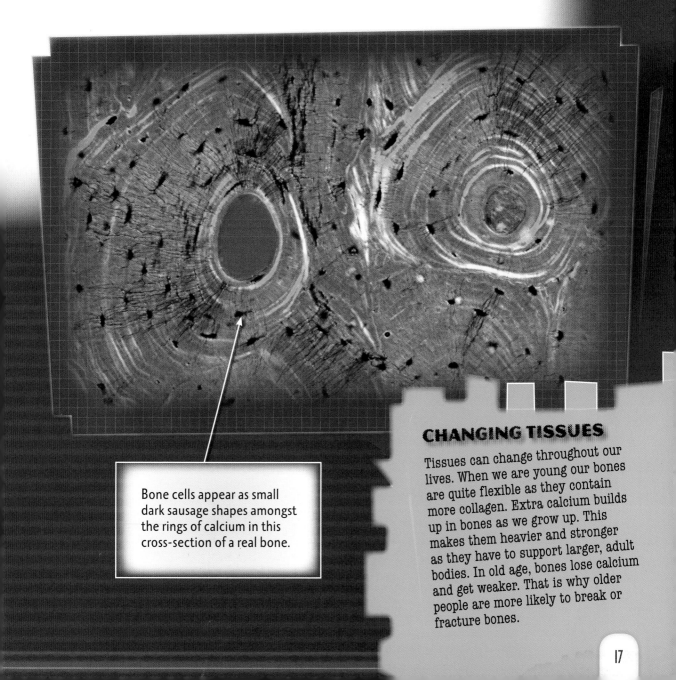

Bone cells appear as small dark sausage shapes amongst the rings of calcium in this cross-section of a real bone.

CHANGING TISSUES

Tissues can change throughout our lives. When we are young our bones are quite flexible as they contain more collagen. Extra calcium builds up in bones as we grow up. This makes them heavier and stronger as they have to support larger, adult bodies. In old age, bones lose calcium and get weaker. That is why older people are more likely to break or fracture bones.

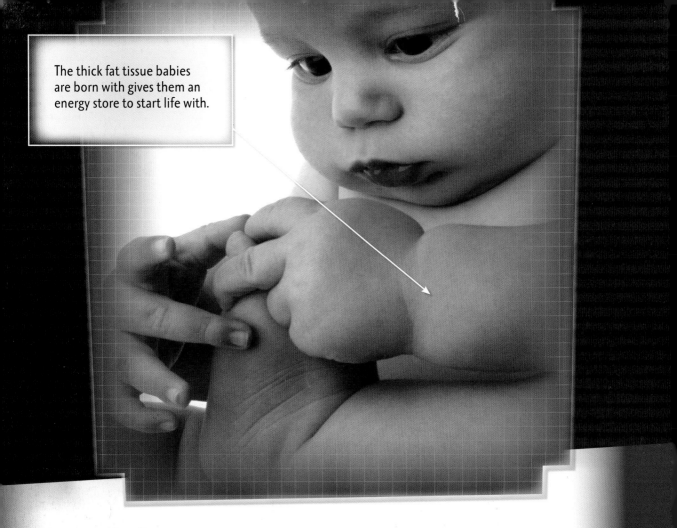

The thick fat tissue babies are born with gives them an energy store to start life with.

Body fat

All of us have some body fat, or adipose tissue, beneath the skin and around important body parts such as kidneys. It is made of cells with a central droplet of fat. The fat is surrounded by a thin ring of cytoplasm containing the nucleus.

Adipose tissue insulates our bodies. This means it stops us losing heat when our surroundings are cold. It cushions body parts from knocks. It is also an emergency energy source. When people do not have enough to eat, their fat cells may break down to make glucose for use in respiration.

THE RIGHT AMOUNT OF FAT

Fat in adipose tissue comes from the food we eat. When people eat more than they need, their bodies make too much fat tissue. The extra weight affects their health, and can cause problems such as heart disease. You should eat only small amounts of fatty food, and do plenty of exercise to stay healthy.

What are organs?

A mountain bike is made up of several separate parts which are made from different materials. For example, it has strong metal wheels with tough rubber tyres. The human machine also contains major parts, called **organs**, with particular jobs to do. Every organ is made of two or more types of tissue that each do part of the organ's work.

Types of organs

There is a wide range of organs in the human body. Some organs are small, such as the pea-sized salivary glands that produce saliva in your mouth. Other organs are big. Your lungs take up most of the space in your chest!

Some organs, such as the brain, are **vital organs**. You could die if these do not work. Other organs, including eyes, help people know the world around them but are not essential for healthy life.

Mountain bikes are made of many parts with different jobs. The rider presses on pedals to move a chain that turns the back wheel and drives the bike. Human organs are parts with different jobs which make the human machine work.

The pump

The heart is a vital organ. Its job is to pump blood around your body all the time. The tissue that does the pumping is made of cardiac, or heart muscle, cells. This squeezes and releases the fist-sized heart around 70 times a minute to make blood flow through it. The cardiac muscle is protected on the outside by a tough tissue with fluid trapped inside. This acts as a cushion, stopping the heart from rubbing against nearby organs as it beats.

Doctors or nurses use a stethoscope to check your heartbeat. It may beat too fast, too slow, or with an uneven rhythm if you are sick.

HEALTHY HEART

Your heart normally beats about 100,000 times every day of your life. You can keep your heart fit by exercising. Regular exercise, such as skipping, running, cycling, and swimming, makes the heart pump faster than usual. This trains the heart to pump using less energy. Then you have more energy to do other things.

Protecting you from the world

The skin is the largest organ of the human body. It makes up around one-fifth of your total weight. The outermost tissue, called the epidermis, is waterproof and protective. It is up to 4 millimetres (0.16 inches) thick on the parts of your body that need most protection from rubbing, such as the soles of the feet.

The layer beneath the epidermis is called the dermis. It contains different tissues including those that make oils to keep your skin from drying up, and hairs to help keep you warm. Neurons, or nerve cells, run through the dermis. They have sensitive endings called receptors that allow your body to feel the world around it, such as the feeling of textures and changes in temperature.

Without a waterproof skin, water could seep between the cells beneath so they could not do their jobs.

Adults make deeper sounds than children because their vocal cords have grown longer. It is rather like the way the long strings on a double bass make deeper sounds than those on a small violin.

Making sounds

The voice box or larynx is the organ we use to talk, sing, whisper, or shout. It is found between your throat and your lungs. The voice box is a ring of cartilage tissue containing two bands of stretchy tissue called vocal cords.

Air you breathe out from your lungs makes the cords flutter back and forward. This makes sound that your mouth shapes into different words or noises. Muscle tissue pulls the cords into different shapes. Vocal cords make higher sounds when they are stretched tight.

ARTIFICIAL ORGANS

Doctors have designed machines that can do part of the work of a faulty organ. Sometimes people get diseases in their throat and have to have their larynx removed. They can then use an artificial larynx that makes the sound they need to talk with.

How do organs work together?

A Formula One car has wheels, an engine, a steering wheel, and many other parts. Each part may be made of several different materials and do a different job. But together the parts enable drivers to race around tracks as fast as possible.

In the human machine there are several **organ systems**. Each is made of several organs that work together to do an important job. For example, your nervous system is made up of the brain, sense organs, and nerves that together allow us to sense the world and control our bodies.

The digestive system

The digestive system breaks down food and absorbs the parts of food, or **nutrients**, required for growing and keeping healthy. It is made up of different organs. For example, the stomach produces chemicals that digest food and the small intestine absorbs nutrients that the body needs.

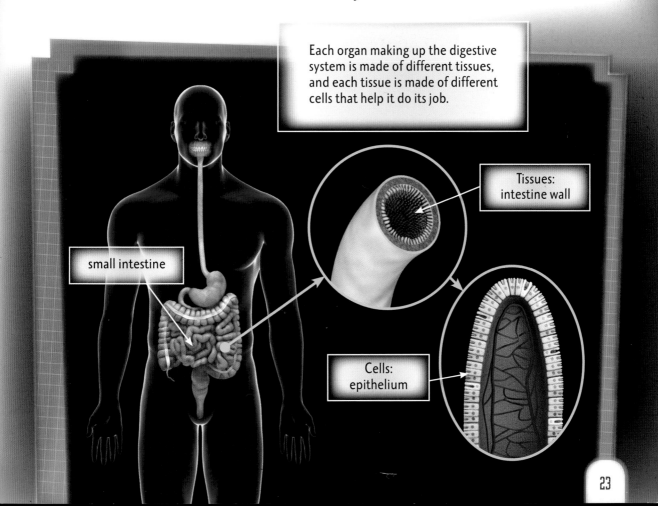

Each organ making up the digestive system is made of different tissues, and each tissue is made of different cells that help it do its job.

Tissues: intestine wall

small intestine

Cells: epithelium

Defending the human machine

The immune system is a set of cells, tissues, and organs all over the body that prevent you from getting sick. Germs such as bacteria often cause diseases and illnesses. Your skin protects most of your body from germs. Germs that get in through your mouth and nose when you eat and breathe may be sneezed or coughed out by sensitive tissues in your throat or lungs. Stomach chemicals kill some germs, but others get into the blood. Here different white blood cells recognize different germs and kill them. White blood cells for the immune system grow in an organ called the spleen, near the stomach.

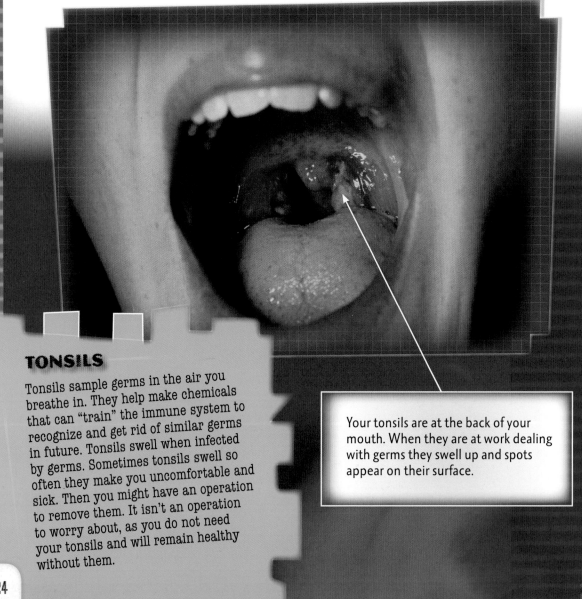

TONSILS

Tonsils sample germs in the air you breathe in. They help make chemicals that can "train" the immune system to recognize and get rid of similar germs in future. Tonsils swell when infected by germs. Sometimes tonsils swell so often they make you uncomfortable and sick. Then you might have an operation to remove them. It isn't an operation to worry about, as you do not need your tonsils and will remain healthy without them.

Your tonsils are at the back of your mouth. When they are at work dealing with germs they swell up and spots appear on their surface.

Systems working together

Different organ systems often need each other to work properly. For example, bones of the skeleton can only move when muscles making up the muscular system pull them. Nutrients produced by the digestive system, such as glucose, need the circulatory system of the blood and heart to get to all the cells in the body's tissues. The circulatory system also needs the respiratory system, as it delivers oxygen from the lungs to the cells.

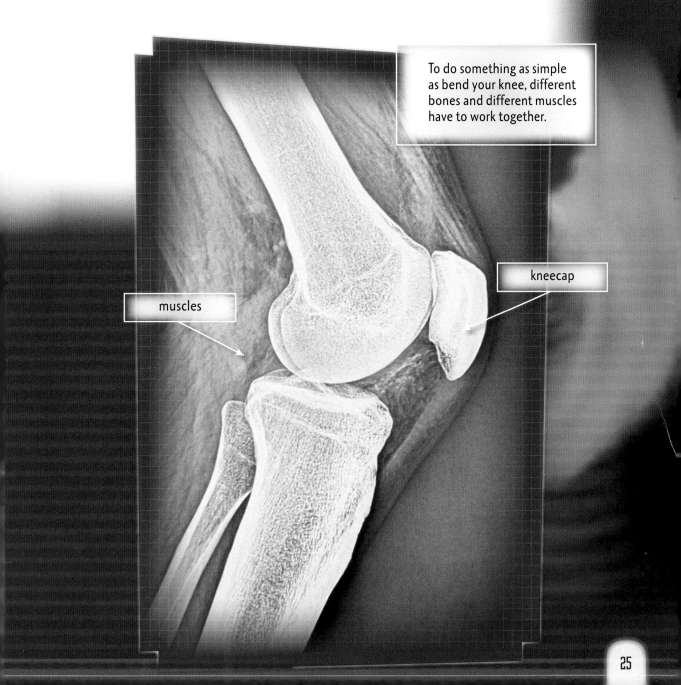

To do something as simple as bend your knee, different bones and different muscles have to work together.

kneecap

muscles

How can I build a healthy body?

You need to look after all the parts making up your body, from cells to organ systems, to keep them healthy and working properly.

A healthy diet

Until you are about 18, your body is growing by making lots of new cells. It is especially important to provide the right nutrients so you grow properly. You need to eat protein such as meat or beans to build cells that make muscle tissue. You need vitamins to keep healthy. For example, vitamin C helps cells live longer and makes your immune system work better. We get vitamin C by eating foods such as oranges and green leafy vegetables.

A balanced diet includes lots of vegetables, fruit, and carbohydrates, such as noodles. Eat proteins and fat in smaller quantities to help stay fit.

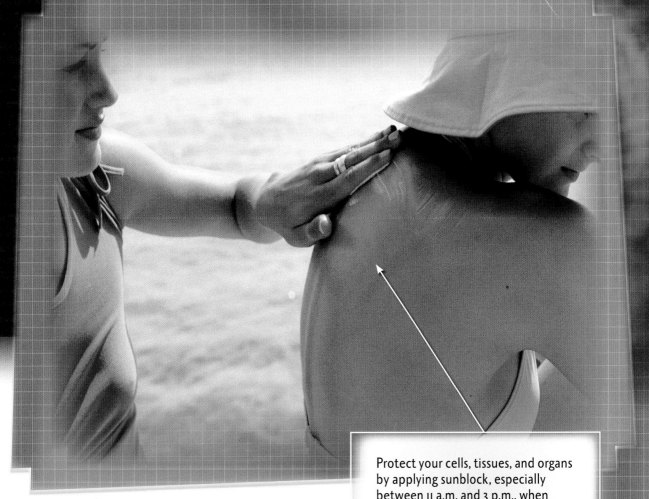

Protect your cells, tissues, and organs by applying sunblock, especially between 11 a.m. and 3 p.m., when sunlight is usually most powerful. This is when sunlight can cause the most harm to your skin.

Energy

You need glucose for energy. An instant intake of glucose from sweets is not a good idea because it all gets into your blood at once. Sugars can also damage your teeth. It is better to eat complex carbohydrates such as potatoes and pasta. Your digestive system digests these slowly, releasing glucose bit by bit. Keep exercising to make sure you use up the energy!

KEEPING SUN SAFE

It is vital to wear sunblock, sun hats, and other protective clothing when it is sunny. Invisible rays in sunlight can make some skin cells divide in an unusual way. This can cause skin cancer, which may be painful, damage the skin permanently, or even cause death.

The world's most complex machine

The human body is often described as the world's most complex machine, but of course it is not really a machine at all. Machines are non-living, mechanical objects, whereas our bodies are natural, living things. But there are similarities. Like a machine, the body is made up of different parts that work together in systems to do particular jobs. These different systems work together to make the whole body – or the human machine – run smoothly and efficiently.

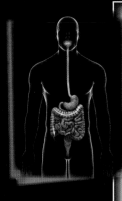

THE SKELETAL SYSTEM

This system of bones supports the other parts of the body, rather as the metal frame of a car supports the vehicle.

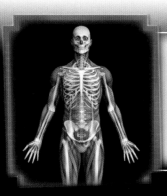

THE DIGESTIVE SYSTEM

The digestive system works as a food-processing machine. It consists of various organs that work together to break down food into forms that the body can use as fuel and raw materials.

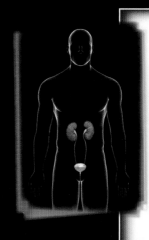

THE EXCRETORY SYSTEM

This is the human machine's waste disposal system, removing harmful substances and waste produced by the other parts of the body.

THE NERVOUS SYSTEM

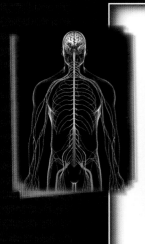

This is the human machine's communication and control system. The brain transmits and receives messages from the senses and the rest of the body. It does this through a network of nerves connected to the brain via the spinal cord.

THE CIRCULATORY SYSTEM

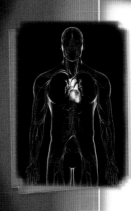

This is the body's delivery system. The heart pumps blood through blood vessels, carrying nutrients and oxygen to the other parts and removing waste from cells.

THE RESPIRATORY SYSTEM

This system provides the rest of the body with the oxygen it needs to get energy from food. It also releases waste gases from the body into the air.

THE MUSCULAR SYSTEM

Muscles are the human machine's motors. Some muscles make the bones of the skeleton move; others work as pumps to keep substances moving through the body.

Glossary

bacteria microscopic living thing. Some bacteria can cause disease.

carbon dioxide gas found in air that is produced when living things release energy from food

cartilage rubbery tissue found, for instance, in the tip of the nose

cell building block or basic unit of all living things. The human body is made up of billions of different cells.

cell membrane thin layer rather like a skin around a cell

chromosome strand, found in a nucleus, that carries instructions about what the cell does

cytoplasm jelly-like material in a cell in which organelles are found

diffusion movement of substance from an area where there is a lot of it to where there is less

digest to break up food into pieces the body can use

divide split in two

energy in science, energy is the ability to do work – to move, grow, change, or to do anything else that living things do

germs living things such as viruses or bacteria that cause illnesses

glucose kind of sugar that the body obtains from carbohydrate foods such as pasta and potatoes

mitochondria organelles in cells where respiration happens

mitosis process in which cells make exact copies of themselves. Mitosis is vital for the growth and repair of all living things.

neuron special cell making up the brain and nerves

nuclear membrane thin layer like a skin around the nucleus

nucleus control centre in a cell

nutrient substance that plants and animals need to grow and survive

organ part of the body made of several tissues that performs a specific function

organelle part of a cell with a particular job to do

organ system group of organs that do a job together, such as the digestive or nervous systems

osmosis special type of diffusion when water moves through tiny holes in a membrane

oxygen gas found in air or in water that many living things use to release energy from glucose

protein type of nutrient found in foods. Meat is a protein, and is vital for the growth and repair of the body.

red blood cell special type of cell for carrying oxygen in the blood to different parts of the body

respiration process by which glucose is combined with oxygen to release energy

tissue group of cells of the same sort, such as skin cells, together doing a job

vital organ organ such as the heart or brain that is essential for life

white blood cell special type of cell in blood that helps the body get rid of germs

Find out more

Websites

At http://vilenski.org/science/humanbody/hb_html/skin.html you can start a human body adventure on the outside of the human body and travel deeper inside, learning about all the organs and body systems.

At http://sln.fi.edu//biosci/systems/systems.html you can learn more about the body systems and the organs they are made up of.

At www.kidshealth.org/kid/body/nails_noSW.html you can get the full story on your nails. The kidshealth site has lots of pages covering blood, skin, hair, muscles, and many other human body topics.

Books

Building Blocks: Cells, Organs and Body Systems, Patricia Macnair (Kingfisher, 2005)

Cells and Systems, Holly Wallace (Heinemann, 2006)

Life Processes, Richard and Louise Spilsbury (Heinemann Library, 2004)

Index